Sacred Solos

Level One

Supplement to All Piano and Keyboard Methods

Compiled, Arranged, and Edited by Wesley Schaum

This series of sacred solos includes favorite hymns, gospel songs, spirituals, and sacred music from the classical repertoire. The selections have been made to appeal to students of all ages and with regard to popularity in different churches. Some of the hymn tunes may be known with different titles and lyrics.

Duet accompaniments offer many possibilities for recitals and Sunday school participation. The duets provide valuable rhythmic training and ensemble experience and are recommended for use at home as well as at the lesson. The person playing the accompaniment may add pedal as desired.

Amazing Grace 7

Beneath the Cross of Jesus 19

Christ the Lord Is Risen Today 5

Hallelujah Chorus *(Handel)*........................16

I Love to Tell the Story 22

Nearer, My God to Thee............................13

Now Thank We All Our God.....................15

Onward, Christian Soldiers.......................20

Praise to the Lord 11

Song of Joy *(Beethoven)* 3

What a Friend We Have In Jesus 9

Performed by Wesley Schaum
Sound engineering by Jeff Schaum

PLAYBACK+
Speed • Pitch • Balance • Loop

To access audio, visit:
www.halleonard.com/mylibrary

5881-6981-8763-3650

ISBN 978-1-4950-8215-3

Schaum

EXCLUSIVELY DISTRIBUTED BY
HAL•LEONARD®

Visit Hal Leonard Online at
www.halleonard.com

Contact us:
Hal Leonard
7777 West Bluemound Road
Milwaukee, WI 53213
Email: info@halleonard.com

In Europe, contact:
Hal Leonard Europe Limited
42 Wigmore Street
Marylebone, London, W1U 2RN
Email: info@halleonardeurope.com

In Australia, contact:
Hal Leonard Australia Pty. Ltd.
4 Lentara Court
Cheltenham, Victoria, 3192 Australia
Email: info@halleonard.com.au

Duet Accompaniment

Notes with *stems up* are to be played with the *right hand*. Notes with *stems down* are to be played with the *left hand*.

Song of Joy

(Ode to Joy)

John W. Schaum

Beethoven

Duet Accompaniment

Christ the Lord Is Risen Today

Charles Wesley   Lyra Davidica

Allegretto

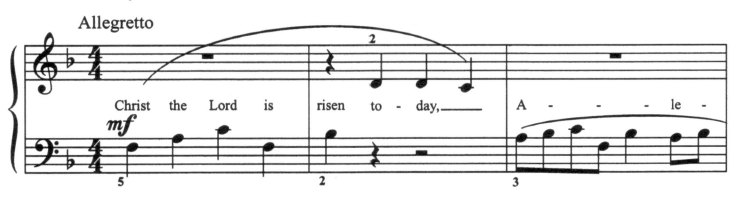

Christ the Lord is risen to - day,____ A - - - le -

lu - ia! Sons of men and an - gels say,____

Al - - - le - lu - ia! Raise your joys and tri - umphs high,

Al - - - le - lu - ia! Sing,__ ye__ heavens, and

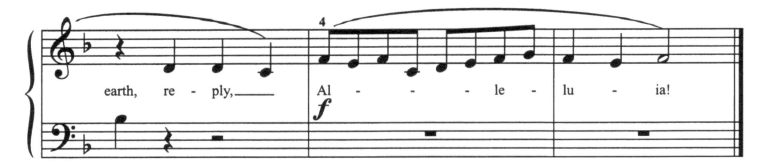

earth, re - ply,____ Al - - - le - lu - ia!

Duet Accompaniment

Amazing Grace

John Newton

Early American Melody

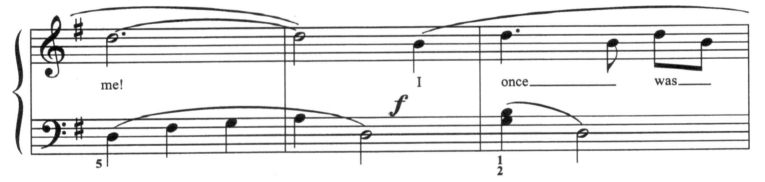

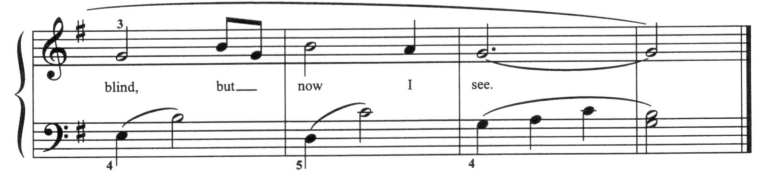

Duet Accompaniment

What a Friend We Have In Jesus

Joseph Scriven

Charles C. Converse

What a friend we have in Je - sus, All our sins and griefs to bear!

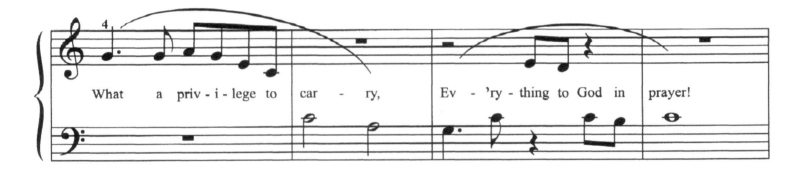

What a priv - i - lege to car - ry, Ev - 'ry - thing to God in prayer!

Oh, what peace we oft - en for - feit? Oh, what need-less pain we bear,

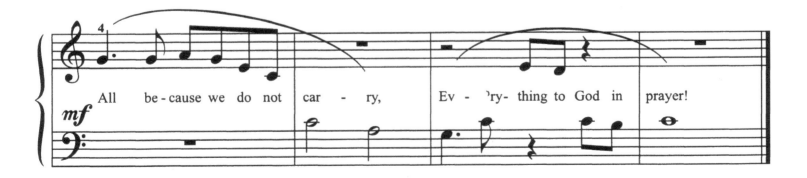

All be - cause we do not car - ry, Ev - 'ry- thing to God in prayer!

Duet Accompaniment

Praise to the Lord

Joachim Neander

Stralsund Songbook

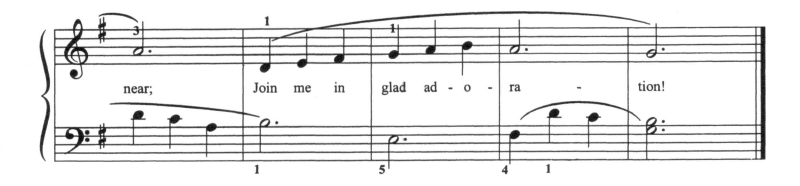

Duet Accompaniment

Nearer, My God to Thee

Sarah F. Adams

Lowell Mason

Tranquillo

Near - er, my God to Thee, Near - er to Thee!

Even tho it be a cross That____ rais - eth me.

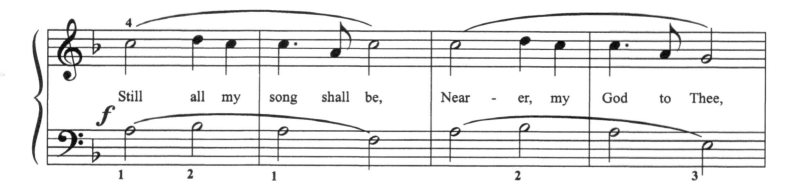

Still all my song shall be, Near - er, my God to Thee,

Near - er, my God to Thee, Near - er to Thee!

Duet Accompaniment

Now Thank We All Our God

Martin Rinkart

Johann Cruger

Andantino

Now thank we all our God, With heart and hands and

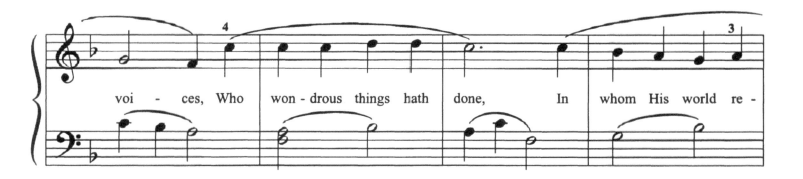

voi - ces, Who won - drous things hath done, In whom His world re -

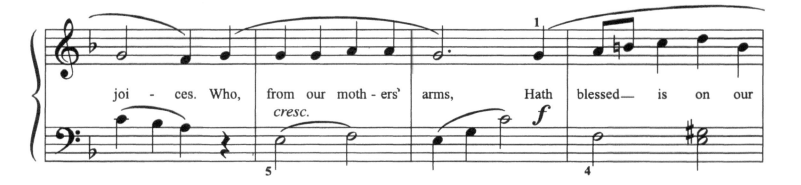

joi - ces. Who, from our moth - ers' arms, Hath blessed— is on our

cresc.

way, With count - less gifts of love, And still is ours to - day.

Hallelujah Chorus

George F. Handel

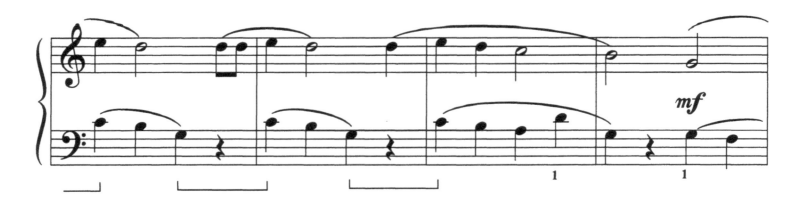

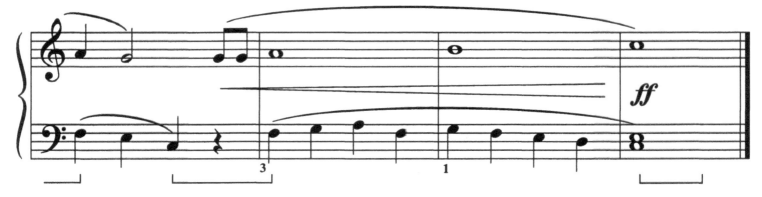

Duet Accompaniment

Beneath the Cross of Jesus

Elizabeth C. Clephane

Frederick C. Maker

Be - neath the cross of Je - sus I fain would take my stand. The shad - ow of a might - y Rock With - in a wea - ry land; A home with - in the wil - der - ness, A rest up - on the way, From the burn - ing of the noon - tide heat, And the bur - den of the day.

Onward, Christian Soldiers

Sabine Baring-Gould

Arthur S. Sullivan

On - ward, Chris - tian sol - diers! March - ing as to war.

With the cross of Je - sus Go - ing on be - fore,

Duet Accompaniment

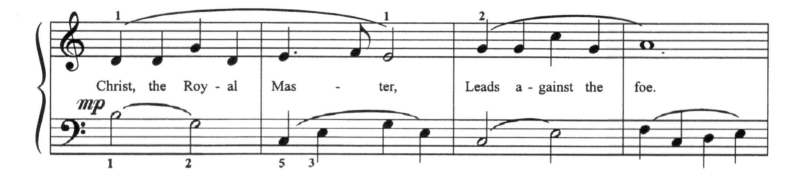

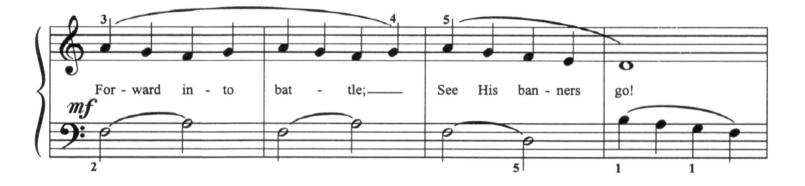

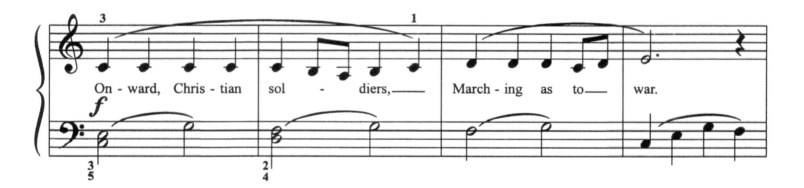

I Love to Tell the Story

Katherine Hankey

William G. Fischer

Moderato

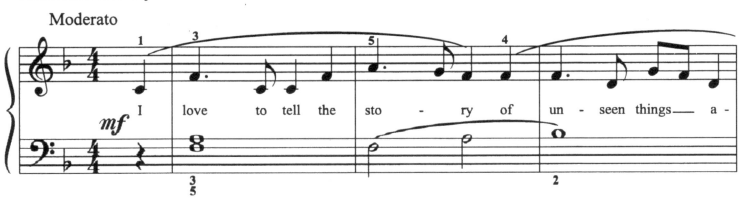

I love to tell the sto - ry of un - seen things— a -

bove, Of Je - sus and His glo - ry, Of—

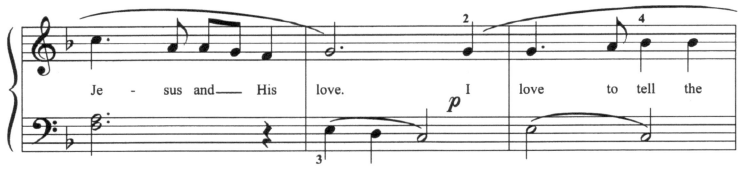

Je - sus and— His love. I love to tell the

Duet Accompaniment

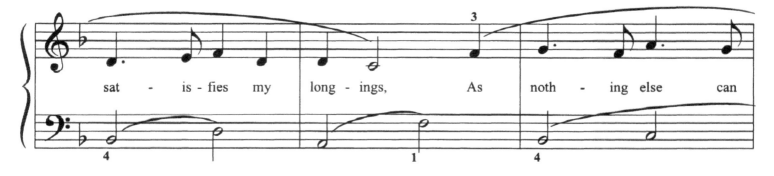

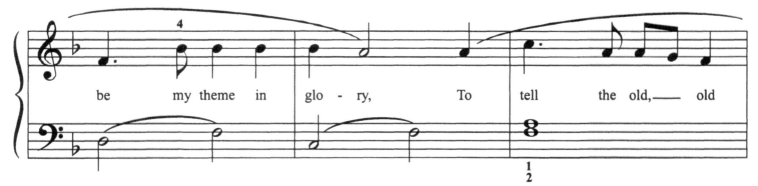

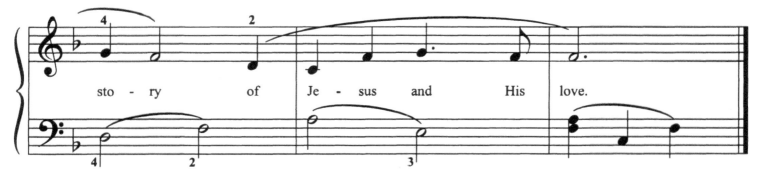